IMAGES
of Wales

MID-RHONDDA

The children of Alaw Nursery School, Trealaw, in 1940. The staff were, from left to right: Miss Martin (teacher), Miss Abigail (headmistress), and Miss Penny (nursery assistant).

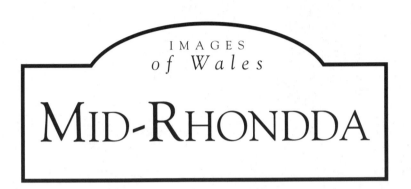

IMAGES
of Wales

MID-RHONDDA

Compiled by
David J. Carpenter

TEMPUS

Tempus Publishing Limited
The Mill, Brimscombe Port,
Stroud, Gloucestershire, GL5 2QG

ISBN 0 7524 1156 X

Typesetting and origination by
Tempus Publishing Limited
Printed in Great Britain by
Midway Clark Printing, Wiltshire

Lower Dunraven Street, Tonypandy, after the Winter storms in 1916, which resulted in the demolishing of power lines and structural damage to buildings.

Contents

Unemployed volunteer miners of Trealaw, working at the 'Don', in 1936.

Foreword

David Carpenter's interest in the Rhondda's past motivates his energetic research and finds expression too in his hunt for period photographs. The present collection is concentrated on Mid-Rhondda, by definition the core of our distinctive community. To him and those like him we owe a debt of gratitude, the young for a picture book showing the way we were, and for some of us, the rousing warmth of recollection, exclaiming 'I remember that!'

The exercise is important for the Rhondda in particular where, in a relatively short period of time, change has been dramatic and unparalleled. Read Malkin's description of the remote, rural, sylvan, sparsely inhabited Llwynypia at the beginning of the nineteenth century and sigh that the camera had still to be invented. Wonder how present-day conservationists would have reacted to the destruction which grounded the mythical squirrel, no longer able to progress, tree to tree, from the lower to the upper limits of the Rhondda and echo Richard Llewellyn's famous book title, *How Green was my Valley*. You will then be shaken with the turmoil of an instant population, exploding from under 1,000 in 1851 to 169,000 after the First World War. The Rhondda was transformed from an area of country folk to one of miners almost to a man, turning the landscape inside out to fuel the age of steam. They are radical, riotous, and religious; respecters of education, pub users and would-be closers, choir members and eisteddfodau competitors, poets and writers; all these people produced a distinctive Rhondda culture.

The Great Depression had a wider impact, yet was felt more acutely here than anywhere in Western Europe. It was a prelude to the complete disappearance of our staple industry, and to conclusive change with hardly a vestige to remind us of the, once ubiquitous, miner. This collection of photographs fills a need in marking the social as well as economic revolution, affecting women as well as their men. The cover recalls aproned housewives, tireless, ever cooking and cleaning, washing clothes on washing days, mangling, and starching, and we can remember them leading grates, polishing brasses, and blue-stoning doorsteps and flagstones 'out the front'. The tools of their daily tasks may now be gone, with a new wave of labour saving appliances, but their work should be recorded for posterity here.

Fortunately, Mid-Rhondda produced, among its talented, a number of home-bred chroniclers, writers and poets, novelists and short story writers such as Lewis Jones and the world famous Rhys Davies of Clydach Vale. Additionally there were those who looked at us from without, such as Jack Jones, Alexander Cordell and Richard Llewellyn.

The greater number of those who made up the Rhondda's instant population came from the Welsh countryside. Welsh was their spoken language. It was the language of culture, of song, and of chapel, but not of the school and education. And these are the people we see in these photographs.

It is obvious that the Welsh language has affected our distinctive Rhondda accent. Its decline has been arrested and its position restored and recognized.

Daeth y rhan fwyaf o'r bobl i'r Rhondda o leoedd gwledig Cymru. Cymraeg oedd yr iaith roedden nhw'n siarad. Cymraeg oedd iaith eu diwylliant, eu caneuon a'r capeli, ond nid iaith yr ysgolion ac addysg. A dyma'r bobl rydyn ni'n gweld yn y lluniau yma.
Mae'n amlwg bod yr iaith Gymraeg wedi effeithio acen arbennig y Rhondda. Mae'n dda i weld does dim ofn arnon ni heddiw o golli'r iaith. Rydyn ni'n clywed yr iaith yn fwy ac yn fwy. Rydyn ni'n sylweddoli pwysigrwydd yr iaith ac yn ei gwerthfawrogi.

I am grateful to David Carpenter for his invitation to write this introduction and to make suggestions regarding the notes accompanying the photographs.

Owen Vernon Jones
JP, BA, BSc, MEd

One

Penygraig and Williamstown

Ely Colliery, opened by the Naval Colliery Company in 1864. In 1908, it became part of the Cambrian Combine, a large mining group headed by D.A. Thomas, later Viscount Rhondda. In 1910, a dispute arose over the opening of a new seam at the pit which contained a large amount of stone and for which the miners claimed extra wages. The row led to the famous Tonypandy Riots. The colliery closed in 1958.

Naval Colliery, Penygraig, c. 1948. The colliery was opened by the Naval Colliery Company in 1875, and the chief partner was Moses Rowland Jnr of Penygraig. The National Coal Board (NCB) closed the colliery in 1958. The site was developed in 1967, and today is the playing field of the Penygraig rugby football club.

The main shopping centre, Tylacelyn Road, Penygraig, in 1911. Note the overhead tram cables.

Police and soldiers were stationed at the Naval Colliery during the strike in December 1910. The soldiers came from the West Riding Regiment, and the policemen were from the Merthyr Borough Force. They were billeted at the Adare Hotel, now known as the Welcome Inn.

Colliers working at Ely Colliery, prior to the strike in 1910.

Residents of Hendrecafn Road celebrating the coronation in 1937.

Mr E. Williams, the saddler from Tylacelyn Road, is seen here exhibiting his range of leather goods during the coronation celebrations for Elizabeth II, in 1953. The other famous saddler in the area was Joby Churchill of Tommy Farr fame. He managed Tommy, whose great fight for the Heavyweight Championship of the World, against Joe Louis, is one of the Rhondda's proudest memories.

Penygraig railway station which served the Ely Valley Railway, in 1937. This station was very popular for Sunday school outings to Barry Island. The line, which has been closed for a long time, was constructed by David Davies of Llandinam for the transporting of coal to Barry Docks.

Nantgwyn Colliery, Penygraig, was sunk by the Naval Colliery Company in 1892. It was closed in 1958, and the site is now occupied by the new Tonypandy Comprehensive School, which was built in 1978.

In 1865, these two cottages housed the original Swan Inn. The landlord at that time was Mr William Roberts.

The rebuilt Swan Hotel, Penygraig, c. 1906. The landlord by this time was Mr Thomas Edward Morris. In later years the pub was renamed the Jolly Collier. It closed in 1961. It was later demolished to provide space for a new road widening scheme in the area. Note the gas lamp to the right which, at night, provided a focus, in every street, for the gathering of children and their games. Ropes, suspended from the arms of the post, made do for swings. Hop scotch could be played in the yellow glow of the lamp.

The, now demolished, White Rock Houses, Dinas Road, Penygraig, *c.* 1900. Note the vicarage in the background.

A GWR wagon delivering goods to the shops in Williamstown, *c.* 1915.

Local dignitaries at the opening of the Penygraig Park on 16 November 1911.

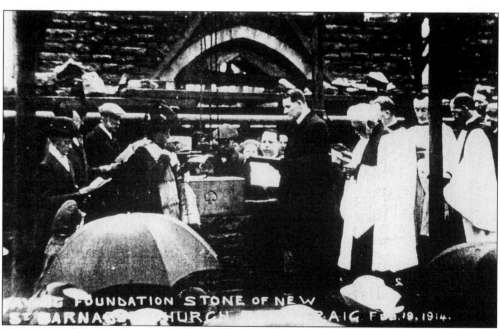

The laying of the foundation stone for St Barnabus' church by Mrs Hughes, the wife of the Bishop of Llandaff, in February 1914.

Harvest festival at St Barnabas' church, *c.* 1920.

Penygraig Park, in 1926. It was built for the local community in 1911, and is still popular today.

The staff and committee of the Penygraig Co-operative Society stores, *c.* 1954. The gentlemen seated in the centre is Mr W.R. Davies, the general manager, and governor of Porth County School. The annual dances were prestigious affairs held at the Park Hotel in Cardiff.

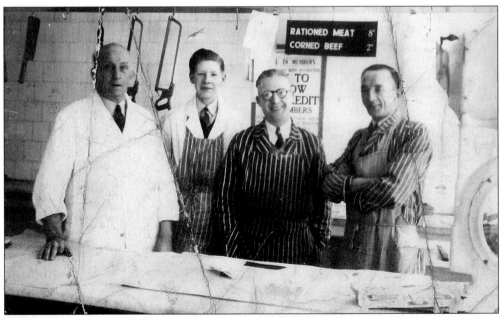

Penygraig Co-operative butcher's department in 1951. The employees at that time were, from left to right: George Lewis (manager), Em Gregory, Don Taylor (a well known businessman, amateur boxer, and friend of Tommy Farr), and Ritchie Phillips.

The Butchers Arms Hotel, in 1906. This hotel was opened in 1861, and its first landlord was Mr Morgan Evan Davies. It closed in the mid 1960s and was demolished because of the road widening scheme in operation at that time.

Penygraig Road, Penygraig, leading to Williamstown, in 1906.

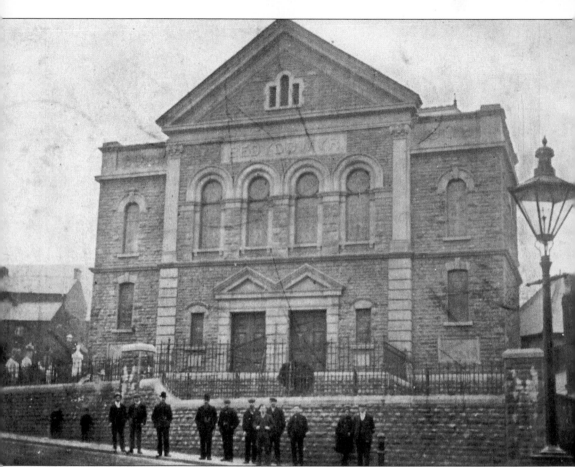

This chapel was built in 1832, and rebuilt in 1858. It was well known for the quality of its singing at the Gymanfa Ganu. However, due to a declining congregation, it closed and remained empty for many years. In 1983, it was taken over by the Penygraig Community Project Group, and converted into a community centre. It houses a community theatre, coffee bar, and recreation rooms and is still going strong today, giving support to the local community.

Mining subsidence at the Co-operative Society stores in 1913.

The Square, Penygraig, in 1908.

Brook Street, Williamstown, *c.* 1910.

Wesley Methodist church, *c.* 1905. This church was built and opened in 1892, and had a seating capacity of 750. Although there was a diminishing congregation, it was ultimately the decision of the church authorities to close the church, and this occurred in March 1967. It remained empty for a number of years, until it was taken over by the Boys' Club Association. After renovation work, it was officially opened by the president of the association, Mr Frankie Vaughan, in October 1974. It has continued to flourish and serves the needs of the youngsters in the local community.

This Welsh Independent chapel was founded in September 1874. It was built and officially opened in August 1876 and its first minister was the Revd J.R. Davies. However, due to declining membership it closed, and was later demolished. The site is now occupied by an old people's home and is called 'Saron Cwrt'.

A view of Soar chapel and the 'Religious Stones', c. 1950.

LLanfair-ar-y-bryn church, in 1905. This church was built in 1889 at a cost of £1500. It held its centenary celebrations on Saturday 13 May 1989, and closed later that month. The vicar at this time was the Revd Stephen Bodycombe. The church and grounds were sold to a building contractor who demolished the church in August 1989. The site is now occupied by five privately owned detached houses.

The shop of Mr G. Moon, a baker, on Blanche Street in 1900. The bakery was situated behind the shop and was able to compete with the large scale bakeries exemplified by the Hopkin Morgan photograph below. The shop front has since been rebuilt and is now a private house.

The delivery cart of Hopkin Morgan bakeries in Blanche Street in 1925.

Williamstown Board School in 1920. This school was built in 1885 and was known as the Williamstown Elementary School. In 1892, it was taken over by the school board and became known as the Williamstown Board School. Its first headmaster, Mr John Jones, was appointed in April 1898.

Williamstown Infants' School, 1935/36.

Williamstown Boys' School choir, winners of the Penygraig and District Welfare Eisteddfod, in September 1927. The conductor was Mr D. Howells.

The bridge connecting Williamstown to Penrhiwfer in the late 1950s. This bridge was commonly known as the 'Black Bridge'. The houses, in the top left, formed Lewis Arms Row, possibly named after the Lewis Arms public house situated further up the slope.

Two
Trealaw

All Saints' church football team, Trealaw, 1950/51. This team were winners of the Ely Valley Cup, and the Rhondda League. The footballer sitting cross-legged to the bottom left is Tom Jones, who later became Mayor of the Rhondda.

Tom John Esq MA, JP (1850 – 1924) was an educationist, philosopher, littérateur, musician and Eisteddfodwyr. He started his career in education in 1872 when he was appointed schoolmaster at the Llwynypia Works School, founded by Archibald Hood. In 1874 he was appointed headmaster of the school and continued in this capacity when the pupils and staff were transferred to the new Llwynypia Mixed School, built in 1896, until he retired in 1910. He was the first Welsh president of the National Union of Teachers, editor of the *Rhondda Leader*, governor of Porth County School and presenter of Salem Congregational church, Llwynypia. Maintaining the family's educational tradition, his brother was the headmaster of the Ynyshir Schools. A bronze plaque in memory of Tom John occupies a prominent position in the main hall of Porth County Comprehensive School.

GENERAL VIEW OF TREALAW. *123*

A view of Upper Trealaw in 1907. Note the empty space, to the middle left, which became the site of the Judges Hall, built in memory of Judge Gwilym Williams of Miskin Manor. It was officially opened by Her Royal Highness, the Princess Louise, accompanied by the Duke of Argyll in July 1909.

A view of Lower Trealaw in 1914. Note the Dinas Arms Hotel and the lodging house immediately behind, to the middle bottom. The lodging house, which was officially called the 'Brithweunydd Workmen's Home', was originally built to accommodate the single men employed at Coffin's Dinas Middle Colliery. Around 1891 it became the Brithweunydd Hotel but reverted back to a lodging house when the licence was transferred to the newly built Dinas Arms in 1906.

Children at play at Ynyscynon Nursery School in 1937.

A carnival at Ynyscynon Road during the coronation celebrations in 1937.

Trealaw Secondary Modern School football team. These players were winners of the Inter Schools Football Team Shield, 1948/49.

The teaching staff at the Trealaw Secondary School, 1948/49. The headmaster at that time was Mr Rhys Jarman who later became a permanent National Union of Teachers representative.

Judges Hall is the shortened version of the full name which was the Judge Gwilym Williams Memorial Hall. It was erected in 1909, in memory of Judge Gwilym Williams of Miskin Manor. Charles Jenkins contractor's of Porth built the hall from the plans of architects A.O. Evans, Williams, and Evans of Pontypridd. The hall cost £6,000 to build and was officially opened by her Royal Highness the Princess Louise, accompanied by her husband the Duke of Argyll, on Friday 23 July 1909. After opening the hall, she was presented with a golden key and a silver casket, containing a 'loyal address of welcome' to mark the occasion. The hall became a popular venue for a variety of activities, including the Friday night boxing matches.

This is the silver casket given to Princess Louise, containing the 'loyal address of welcome' from the people of Mid-Rhondda. The casket was presented to Her Royal Highness on behalf of the Mid-Rhondda Chamber of Trade by its president Mr L.W. Llewellyn.

The bridge connecting Tonypandy with Trealaw, July 1937. Note the poster, on the left, on the wall of the Judges Hall, advertising a forthcoming boxing match.

Trealaw Hotel in 1910. The landlord at that time was Mr George Wells. The hotel was built in 1875 and its first landlord was Mr Frederick Harris. It was regularly used by commercial travellers who took advantage of the new railway station which opened in Tonypandy in 1908. At that time the hotel was popularly known as 'Paddy's Goose'.

Miskin Road and the Miskin Hotel in 1905. The landlord at this time was Mr David C. Evans. The hotel was built in 1875 and its first landlord was Mr Robert Williams. It is still popular with the local community.

The Royal Hotel, c. 1910. This hotel was built in 1895 and its first landlord was Mr Jenkin Williams. The canopy over the entrance was moved in the 1940s. This is another hotel that is still popular with the local community.

Maesyffynon House, *c.* 1910. In 1889, Maesyffynon Farm was a single story building with a thatched roof and was leased by Mr John David Watkin from Judge Gwilym Williams of Miskin Manor. It was purchased around 1905 by the Davies family who were wealthy brewers. They carried out extensive building work on the farmhouse, and even added a second storey. When complete, the whole construction was renamed Maesyffynon House. In 1920 the house was bought by Mr Montague Williams, who sold it to Mr William Bethuel Heycock in 1930. In 1965 Mr William Bethuel Heycock sold off a large amount of the grounds for the development of private houses and bungalows.

All Saints' church ladies bowling club, 1937/38. The vicar at that time was the Revd W.H.H. Williams MA.

Maes-Yr-Haf, known as Summer Meadow, in 1910. This was a large Victorian stone building set in two acres of land and was the residence of Mr David Melville Davies and Mrs Alice Florence Davies. In April 1927, it was sold to William and Emma Noble, who were members of the Society of Friends. They purchased, repaired, decorated, and refurbished it, at a cost of £1,750. They then opened it to give support to the social and educational needs of local unemployed men and their families.

Maes-Yr-Haf choir on their visit to Denmark where they sang before the Danish Royal family in 1936.

Clydach Court, c. 1910. Clydach Court was built around 1905 and was owned by Mr John David Williams, a relative of Mr David Williams, the colliery owner who was known under the bardic name of 'Alaw Goch'. In 1928 it was taken over by the Rhondda Urban District Council Education Committee for the primary purpose of teaching commercial subjects, although other subjects were also taught. In 1964 it was demolished, and an old people's residential home was built at a cost of £101,274. The home, which could accommodate sixty residents, was officially opened by the Rt Hon. James Griffiths, Secretary of State for Wales, on 19 December 1964 and is still in use today.

The van of Mr Edgar Seale, dairyman, of Evans Terrace, in 1935. This ex-post office van was brought for the princely sum of £10! The driver was Mr Ivor Warnell and the delivery man was Mr Bernard Blake.

The Trealaw and District juvenile choir, after their concert called *Twin Sisters* at the Judges Hall in 1931.

The 1st Trealaw Girl Guides troop in 1931.

Construction of the 'Don' unemployment club in 1936. When this club was completed, it allowed unemployed miners to pursue such activities as shoe repairing, carpentry, and furniture making. There were drama groups and physical training, as well as a wireless set on which the BBC broadcast special programmes for musical listening and discussion groups, in which they were able to participate.

Unemployed miners at a listening session in the cellar of the partly built 'Don' in April 1935.

The children of Charles Street in 1931. On the back row, from left to right: Eddie Owen, Albert Blinkton, Glyn Owen, Charlie Lester, -?-. On the second row from the back: Sam Hughes, Ron Griffiths, -?-, Dai Hughes, Elwyn Bryant, -?-, John Blinkton. On the third row: Sam Lloyes, -?-, Thelma Lester, Des Squelch, Mal Griffiths, Frank Bryant, Viv Raymond. On the front row: Glyn Hughes, -?-, -?-, -?-, Thelma Blinkon, Billy Lester, Trefor Griffiths, Ray Squelch, Ken Bryant.

The cemetery was named Llethr-Ddu after the cottages which were situated near the gates. It was officially opened in 1882, although the first burial took place in 1881. The church was also built in 1881, but in later years the high steeple was removed because it would not stand up to high winds; a smaller counterpart was built and can be seen today.

Brithweunydd Road, Trealaw, in 1905.

Residents of Brithweunydd Road celebrating Victory in Europe with a street party in 1945.

Bute Rovers in 1921. On the back row, from left to right: Ben Jones, F. Burridge, James Holloway, D. Moreton, Sid Studley, -?-, Alf Donnelly. On the front row: Reg Bridge, Geof Bennett, Arthur Jones, Ben Marshall, Vince Donnelly.

Trealaw Central Club and Institute football team in 1922. The club is now known as the Trealaw Social Working Men's Club and Institute, but is popularly called the 'Res', due to its close proximity to the cemetery, and the cemetery gates!

Three
Tonypandy

A temperance rally outside St Andrew's church, Tonypandy, in 1916.

The new railway station at Tonypandy and Trealaw showing the first train to enter the station in 1908.

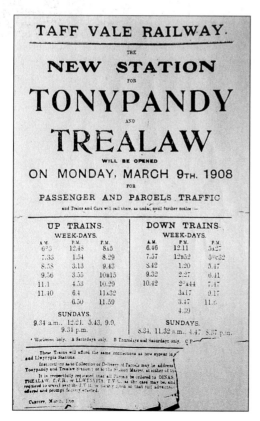

A poster issued in the locality announcing the opening of the station in March 1908.

Trinity chapel, Tonypandy, *c.* 1906. This chapel was built on the site of two cottages and was opened in March 1889. The first pastor was the Revd Christmas Lewis, who took over in November 1889. Due to the increase in size of the congregation, four more cottages were demolished, and the building of the new chapel began in 1893. The building was not completed until 1904 and when it opened the pastor was the Revd F.W. Cole.

Central Hall, in 1948. This magnificent building was built in 1923 to replace a smaller chapel which had previously stood on the site. The new building was originally known as the Wesleyan Central Hall but in later years its name was changed to the Methodist Central Hall.

Dunraven Street, Tonypandy, *c*. 1907. Note the wasteland at the end of the shops on the left; this later became the site of the Empire Theatre, which opened in November 1909. On Saturday night this street was always packed with pedestrians and was known locally as the 'Pandy Parade'. Trade was brisk and the shopkeepers were prosperous.

Lower Dunraven Street, *c.* 1906.

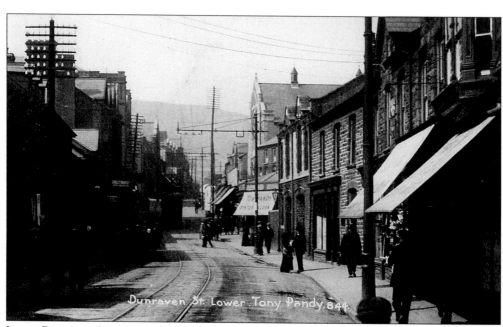

Lower Dunraven Street in 1915. Note the tram in the distance.

The Dunraven Hotel in Lower Dunraven Street in 1923.

Workmen engaged in the construction of the New Empire Theatre of Varieties which was completed in 1909. Its official opening took place on 12 November 1909.

The Empire Theatre, and the newly built Cross Keys Hotel, *c.* 1912.

The Tonypandy County Club, Primrose Street, *c*. 1905. Note the large library sign in the window, making an unspoken claim that the club was not just for drinking but also for edification, which gave it a stamp of respectability. It closed during the first World War.

Primrose Street, Tonypandy, *c.* 1910. The school on the left was, for many years, the home of the Tonypandy Youth Club.

Tonypandy Youth Club were winners of the Collins Cup at the Mid-Rhondda youth clubs annual sports event in 1947. The warden of the youth club at that time was Mr 'Bill' Griffiths. At the back, from left to right: John Isaacs, Norman 'Nobby' Baker. On the second row from the back: Derick Clothier, Idris John, David Jones, Gorden Moore, Roy Jones, Mr Smith (groundsman). On the third row: Howard John, Ken Soper, Randall Lewis, Len Meredith, Rees Clements, Gwyn Evans, Gwyn Jones, Desmond Barnett, Ray Pope, Spencer Evans, Sid Anthony. On the fourth row: Connie Moore, Peggy Clarke, Jeanette Warnell, Merrill Jenkins. On the front row: Ann Meredith, Mrs E. Rees, Judy Powell, -?-.

MID-RHONDDA A. F. C. (MUSHROOMS.)

BACK ROW:-PATTISON, JONES, MOODY, BAIN, McCULLUM, OSBORNE.
FRONT ROW:-HOPKINSON, SEED, CARMICHAEL, BACHE, GOODWIN.

Mid-Rhondda AFC (Mushrooms), *c*. 1925. The team was well known throughout the Rhondda at this time as 'The Mush'. It was formed just after the First World War and played at the Mid-Rhondda Welfare Ground. Their popularity was highlighted by the large crowds who attended their matches. Many of their players went on to international status. In 1927, they played an exhibition match against Cardiff City, who had won the FA Cup that year, and the crowds were overflowing the ground. The match ended in a draw. Later, it would appear, 'The Mush' were refused entry into the Welsh league of that year.

Coronation celebrations at Primrose Street, Tonypandy, in 1937.

Tonypandy Infants' School - Nursery Class 1937.

Children at Tonypandy Infants School in 1937. This school celebrated its centenary in 1996.

The Cross Keys Hotel, in 1919. The original Cross Keys was built in 1861 and was nothing more than a tin shed. Its landlord at this time was Mr William Sherra. The New Cross Keys was built around 1909.

Dunraven Street, Tonypandy, c. 1925. This was a time when the horse and cart had to compete with the trams, but thankfully not with the cars or buses of today.

Tonypandy and Trealaw Free Library in Dunraven Street, Tonypandy. It was established by a group of local businessmen in 1899.

Maesyffrwd House Tonypandy, *c.* 1912. The house was used for many years as the vicarage for St Andrew's church. When the new vicarage was built in the grounds of the church, the house was sold and today is a private residence. It is now known as Compton House.

The premises of J. Owen Jones, milliner's, with its staff in 1923.

Dunraven Street, Tonypandy, *c.* 1910. The new market was situated near the site of the present day Barclays Bank.

Tonypandy Higher Elementary School, *c.* 1920. This school was built in 1915, and was originally formed to prepare its students for clerical jobs. It became a secondary school in January 1922, and part of the comprehensive system in the late 1960s. Unfortunately, it closed in 1991, and all the students were transferred to the new comprehensive school at Penygraig. The building was demolished in 1994 and the site was converted into a large car park for the benefit of the shoppers in Tonypandy in 1995.

The male staff of Tonypandy Secondary School in July 1940. On the back row, from left to right: Ben 'Big' Evans, Johnny 'Lat' Thomas, Brynmor Jones, J.R. Davies, Horace 'Blondie' Jenkins. On the middle row: -?-, -?-, Charlie Pierce, Edward Hugh, 'Ego' Davies, William 'Froggy' Jones. On the front row: -?-, Evan 'Ianto' Jones, ? White, R.R. 'Gafer' Davies, Owen Hughes.

Dunraven Street, Tonypandy in 1904. Note the empty building spaces in the middle and to the left of the telegraph pole.

The delivery cart of G. Milton, grocer's, outside their shop, *c.* 1910.

Dunraven Street, Tonypandy in 1910. Note the tramcar in the centre of picture and the overhead cables.

The Pandy All Blacks football team, 1921/22. Only some of the players can be named: Buller Mills, seated fifth from the left; Jack Atkins, on the second row from the back, first on the left, Arthur Lloyd, on the second row, sixth from the left; Marsh Haddock, on the second row, fourth from the left and Dick Granville in the centre of the second row. The mascot, sat on the floor, in the bottom right, is Iorrie Lloyd. The gentlemen, sat to the right of the trophy table is Mr Sam Wiltshire, owner of Sam Wiltshire's sports shop, Dunraven Street, Tonypandy.

Some of the staff outside Peglers' Stores Ltd in Dunraven Street, Tonypandy, *c.* 1930. This store served the local community for many years, but eventually closed due to competition with the supermarkets.

Bridgend Hotel, *c*. 1940. The hotel was built in 1875 and its first landlord was Mr John Llewellyn. Despite being popular in the early 1940s, it closed in 1958 and remained empty for a number of years. It was then demolished and the site landscaped; it has now become the new location for the cenotaph.

Dunraven Street, Tonypandy, in 1904. Note the absence of traffic!

A squad of the Tonypandy Home Guard in 1940.

The Woollen Mill is known locally as the Fulling Mill, and is the foundation for the name of Tonypandy, which means the lay or land of the Fulling Mill. It was opened by Mr Harri David in 1738, and worked continuously, treating wool for the local population for many years. However, with the importation of cheaper cloths into the valleys it was unable to compete and was forced to close in 1914. Its owner at the time was Mr David Evans. Unsuccessful attempts were made to dismantle the looms and the water wheel for the National Museum of Wales.

De Winton Street, Tonypandy, in 1905.

The Boys' Brigade's annual parade through De Winton Street, Tonypandy in 1906. The Old Mill is situated below the wall on the right.

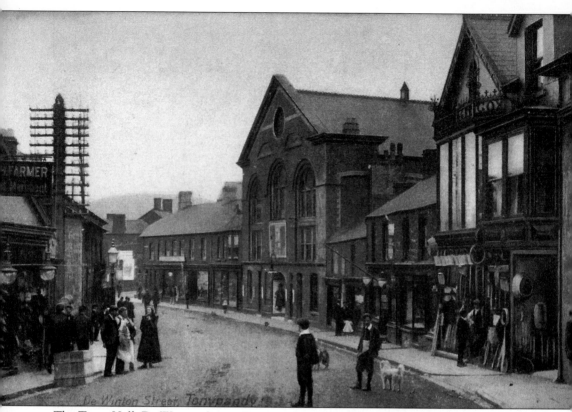

The Town Hall, De Winton Street, Tonypandy, was built in 1892, and became a theatre when it was taken over by Mr Will Stone. The Theatre Royal, as it was known, became famous for its variety acts and Charlie Chaplin was said to have performed there in his pre-Hollywood days. The Bioscope was introduced in 1910 and proved popular with the local community. In later years, the hall was used by many amateur organizations for the production of plays and concerts. It closed during the war years and never reopened.

A tramcar in De Winton Street, Tonypandy, c. 1912. The all-metal bridge behind the tramcar was replaced during the construction of the new Tonypandy bypass in 1987.

Members of Moriah Welsh Baptist chapel after their concert at the Theatre Royal, Tonypandy, in 1938. The minister at that time was the Revd Washington Owen. Concerts such as these demanded regular practising, as well as elaborate scenery and costumes made by the mothers of the cast.

Tonypandy Youth Club's 'Rag', in 1950. Could this be the Rhondda's first attempt at the land speed record?

A float depicting the costumes of 'All Nations' in the 'Rag' of 1950.

The 'Atomic Comet', the Rhondda's answer to cruise missiles, 1950.

On the 28 October 1909, Mr W. Abraham (Mabon) MP unveiled a drinking fountain erected in memory of the late Archibald Hood JP, founder of the Glamorgan Colliery. It was purchased out of the surplus monies collected for the magnificent statue situated in the grounds of the Workman's Institution in Llwynypia. The fountain, which is 13 ft high, was built of cast iron on a pedestal of Aberdeen granite, and surmounted by an Egyptian water carrier supporting a powerful gas lamp. It has three drinking taps, one cattle trough, and two dog troughs. It was designed by Mr R.S. Griffiths, an architect from Tonypandy and was built by the Coalbrookdale Company in Shropshire. It bears the following inscription, 'This fountain is erected in conjunction with the statue at the Workman's Institution, by the workmen of Llwynypia Colliery and others, as a memorial to the late Archibald Hood Esq JP and founder of the Llwynypia Colliery'. There was also a Welsh inscription, 'Y cyfiawn a fydd am fywyf ei anifail' which translated into English reads, 'The just/righteous are careful/caring about the lives of their animals'. The fountain was relocated, many years later, in Tonypandy Square to form an island around which the traffic flowed. It was then commonly known as 'The Eros of the Rhondda'. Unfortunately, it was badly damaged in a collision and was removed to the local council yard in September 1968.

Tonypandy Square, *c.* 1915.

The official unveiling of the drinking fountain in memory of the late Archibald Hood JP by William Abraham (Mabon) MP, in 1909. The crowds that gathered provide proof of the popularity of this coal owner.

VISIT OF PRINCE & PRINCESS ALEXANDER OF TECK
TO TONYPANDY APRIL 21 1914

Miss Sibyl Llewellyn, daughter of Mr Leonard W. Llewellyn ME, presenting Princess Alexandra of Teck with a magnificent bouquet of flowers provided by the Glamorgan Colliery officials during her visit to Tonypandy in April 1914. Mr Leonard was later knighted for his contribution to the war effort and sired the famous Sir Harry Llewellyn, Olympic gold medalist, and owner of Foxhunter, his equally famous horse with whose name he is always coupled.

J.R. Evans, grocer's, Tonypandy Square in 1905.

Boarded up shops in De Winton Street, Tonypandy, after riots during the 1910 strike.

Boarded up shops in Tonypandy Square after the riots and raids.

Tonypandy Square, in 1910. Horse drawn 'taxis', known as brakes, were used to transport people around the valley and were the only form of transport which could reach Clydach Vale, because of the steepness of the ascent from the floor of the valley.

A view from Tonypandy Square in 1931. This view shows the relocated 'Lady with the Lamp' acting as a traffic island.

A march through Tonypandy, protesting against the hardship caused during the 1921 strike.

The opening of the Co-operative stores, Tonypandy, in June 1914. The Co-op shared the grocery trade in the Rhondda with Peglers' and Thomas and Evans, which were the Rhondda's other multiple stores.

Jerusalem chapel was built in 1872. Due to a diminishing congregation, it was demolished in 1983. A block of flats was built on the site in 1984.

Berw Road, Tonypandy, *c.* 1940. The building on the right was called the Llwynypia Social and Non-Political Club, but was commonly known as 'The Greasy Waistcoat'. It closed in April 1939, and was used for a short while for the billeting of American soldiers, during the Second World War.

The Thistle Hotel, Tonypandy, c. 1950. This was so named because of its proximity to the 'Scotch' Colliery and Llwynypia's 'Scotch Terraces'. All of these terraces have names reminiscent of Scotland which gives a clear indication that the local owner, Archibald Hood was of Scottish origin.

A view of Upper Tonypandy in 1909.

Four
Clydach Vale

The Central Hotel, Clydach Vale, *c.* 1920. It was built in 1901 and today is a popular venue with the local community. Opposite, on the left, is the Royal Stores, home of Rhys Davies, the internationally acclaimed writer of short stories and novels. In his autobiographical *Print of a Hare's Foot,* he describes a battle between the police and strikers on the steps of the Central Hotel, as observed from his bedroom window, 'crammed with yelling strikers armed with sticks and mandrels, the road rose to my eyes. Policemen, far outnumbered, bounded among the rioters with batons drawn. The horses reared, their riders, one hand kept firmly on the reins, flayed long switches on the rioters'.

The laying of new drains and the construction of the lower manhole shaft at the Blaenclydach culvert in March 1939.

Cambrian Male Voice Choir, prior to their departure from the NUM Club, Tonypandy. This was their first overseas tour of Germany in 1974.

A Rhondda transport bus, negotiating the corner of Thomas Street and Berw Road, Blaenclydach, in 1922. Before this bus service, Clydach was too steep to be negotiated by tramcars, and brakes were the only public transport. The brake service to the railway station was organised by Will Owen.

A view of the Royal Hotel from Thomas Street in 1910.

The Royal Hotel, *c.* 1920. The hotel was opened in 1895 and its first landlord was Mr Peter Thomas. It closed in 1961, and became a Boys' Club in 1962. The Boy's Club closed around 1986 and the building was demolished as part of the Tonypandy bypass scheme.

Clydach Road, Blaenclydach, in 1922.

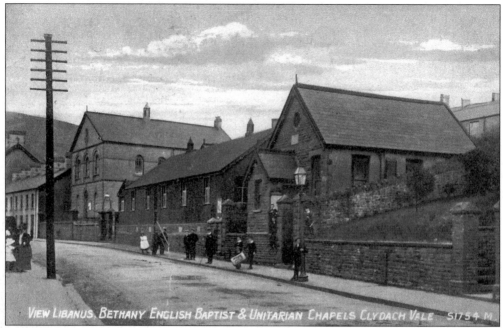

Libanus, Bethany and Bethlehem chapels on Clydach Road in 1904. Due to a falling congregation, Libanus chapel was later converted to the Clydach Vale Boys' Club. Bethany chapel still has a strong congregation of worshippers, while Bethlehem chapel, which was built 1895, has been taken over by Noddfa chapel.

Blaenclydach and Clydach Vale Conservative Club, c. 1910. This club was formally opened on 9 May 1908 and had originally been a dwelling house. The first committee was made up of: Mr W.D. Jones (chairman), Mr T. Evans (vice chairman), Mr Rees (treasurer), and Mr Myrddin Thomas (secretary). The membership at that time numbered 110. Only people who held with 'Conservative principles and were of good character' were allowed to be members. The steward appointed at that time was Mr Edward Evans.

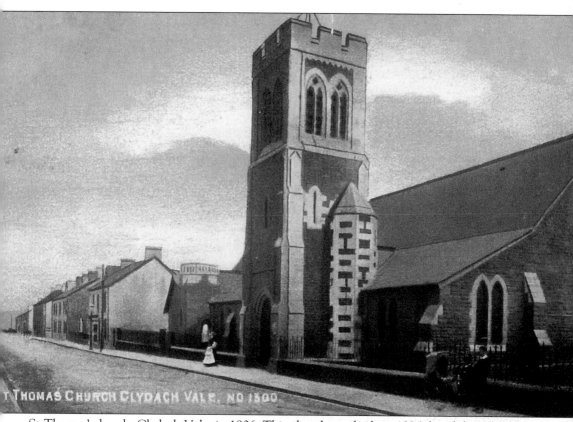

St Thomas' church, Clydach Vale, in 1906. This church was built in 1896, but did not have a permanent vicar until 1908. He was the Revd William Meredith Morris and stayed until 1921. The church celebrated it centenary in 1996.

Bush Houses, Clydach Vale, *c.* 1920. These houses were built to accommodate the miners and their families when the Cwm Clydach Colliery opened in 1864, and were originally called the Cwm Clydach Cottages. They were later renamed Bush Houses, but were known locally by the nickname, 'White City'.

Blaenclydach Colliery, *c.* 1915. This colliery was known locally as the 'Gorki Drift Mine' and was opened around 1912. Note the abandoned winding gear in the background which belonged to Cwm Clydach Colliery which closed around 1895.

Workers dismounting from the 'Spake' of the 'Gorki Drift Mine', after finishing their shift in the 1930s. The overman, on the extreme right, was Mr Ernie Trotman and the haulier was Mr Evan White, on the extreme left.

Cwm Clydach School, Standard 4, in 1891. Mr R.R. Williams, a student teacher at the school, later became its headmaster and received the Albert Medal 2nd Class for bravery during the terrible floods of 1910.

A reunion of the same Standard 4 class, in 1935. In 1931, Mr R.R. Williams, in the centre, behind the kneeling gentleman, had resigned and was the Director of Education for the Rhondda.

On 11 March 1910, an accumulation of water of approximately 800,000 gallons burst out of an abandoned level causing the deaths of six people and a tremendous amount of damage to property.

The flood water rushed into the grounds of this school and caused the deaths of three school children. The flood resulted in a tremendous amount of damage to the school and the surrounding area.

The children of Cwm Clydach School preparing for the funerals of the victims of the flood, which took place on Wednesday 16 March 1910.

The people of Clydach Vale gathered for the funeral of the flood victims.

Wern Street children's carnival, celebrated the coronation of Elizabeth II in 1953.

The children of Cwm Clydach school took part in a play called *The Blue Prince* at Clydach Vale Assembly Hall in 1949.

The residents of Wern Street celebrated the Festival of Britain at the Clydach Vale Assembly Hall in 1951.

The Square, Clydach Vale, *c.* 1910. Soar chapel is on the left, while Calfaria chapel is in the top right. At middle right is the Clydach Vale Hotel, which opened in 1884. Its landlord at the time was David John Williams.

Clydach Vale Library, in 1906. It was built in 1880, and officially named the Cambrian Colliery Library and Institute. The cost of maintaining the library was met by the miners at the local Cambrian Colliery who contributed $\frac{1}{2}$ d per week from their wages. Unfortunately, due to unemployment problems which occurred from 1918 onwards, contributions ceased, with the result that the library closed around 1926. The building was later demolished.

Soar chapel, Clydach Vale, in 1906. The Revd Thomas Williams served as pastor to this chapel for twenty-five years. Due to falling numbers in the congregation, the chapel closed and is now an old people's home.

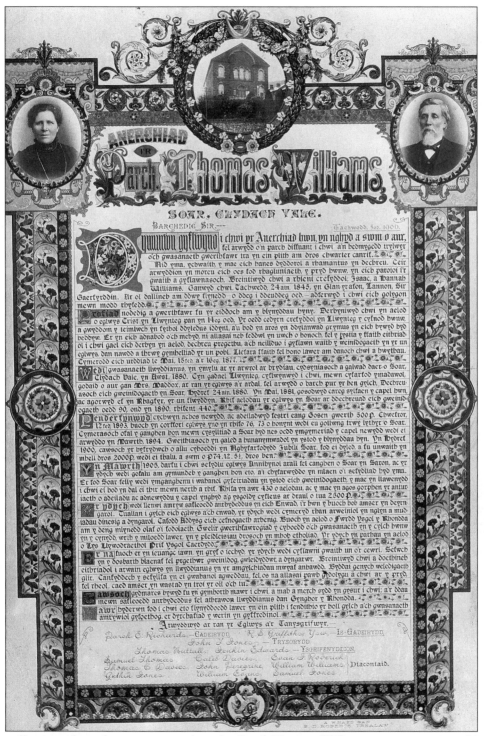

An illuminated parchment presented to the Revd Thomas Williams in appreciation of his services to Soar chapel from 1880 to 1905.

Cambrian Colliery, Clydach Vale, *c.* 1907. The No. 1 shaft was sunk in 1872 and during its life was the scene of two major explosions. The first was in 1905, when thirty-three miners lost their lives and the second was in 1965, when thirty-one miners lost their lives. This was the last major explosion to take place in the Rhondda.

Dai Morgan's slaughter house was set alight during the strike riots of 1910. Rumour had it that the owner was a police informer.

Five

Llwynypia

An aerial view, showing the Glamorgan 'Scotch' Colliery with the famous 'Scotch Terraces' in the background, c. 1900.

The Thistle Hotel and the main road leading to Tonypandy, *c.* 1915.

A house called Hillside, Llwynypia, in 1906. Around 1970, a part of the large grounds was sold off and modern bungalows were built.

This was the combined scholarship class of Llwynypia school, seen with the headmaster, Mr R.D. Lewis, in 1942/43. They were a successful class and among them were, in later life, three doctors, two surgeons, one solicitor, three headmasters, one chartered engineer and one minister of religion.

Archibald Hood realized the value of education, and was aware of the shortcomings within the miners' families. Therefore, in 1869, he set up a school at No. 1 Ayton Terrace, to educate the sons and daughters of his workers. The intake at that time was about twenty-four mixed pupils, and the first schoolmaster was Mr Gumley. Due to demand, a new school was built and opened in 1872 which was known as the Llwynypia Works or Colliery School. This school flourished for many years until the building of the Llwynypia Board School in 1896, when all the pupils were transferred there.

Llwynypia Mixed School, *c.* 1906. This is the school that replaced the one built by Archibald Hood in 1872 and mentioned above.

Llwynypia Mixed School won the cup at the Mid-Rhondda sports contest, 1938/9. On the back row, from left to right: David Thomas, -?-, Colin ?, Elwyn Jones, Billy Westacott, Billy Emanuel, Raymond Howells, Raymond Thomas, Dennis Hughes, Dennis Shaw, Dennis James. On the second row from the back: Viv ?, Bronwen Clarke, Margaret ?, Jean Parker, Margaret Thomas, Sheila Jones, Gwynneth Province, Kitty Samuels, Nancy Nixon, Peggy Rees, Elsie Pike, Delores James, Gordon Evans. On the third row: Doreen Jones, Jean Houston, -?-, Doreen Davies, Nan Province, Mr Bowen (headmaster), Iris Howells, Marion Lewis, Glenys Cox, Jean Jones, Eileen Davies, Marion Churchill. On the from row: Ron Samuels, David Pinkham, -?-, Jeff Spickett, Rhys Clements, Lesley Carpenter, Trevor Evans, Bernard Hall, Gwilym ?, Arthur Sibley.

Llwynypia Infants' School in 1904. This school took over from the Llwynypia Colliery School and represented state education as distinct from denominational schools and schools financed by the philanthropy of the local mine owner. Increasingly, teachers were college trained, but 'uncertificated' teachers taught in Rhondda schools throughout the 1920s.

Mixed pupils of Class 2B at Llwynypia Infants' School in 1913.

Llwynypia House, in 1906. The house had been used for many years as a social club by the local miners and their families and while its official title was The Cambrian Lodge NUM Social Club and Institute, it was known locally as 'The Pick and Shovel'.

The Llwynypia division of the St John's Ambulance Brigade in October 1947. Classes, under the guidance of superintendents Thomas Roberts and Thomas Matthews, were held on Friday evenings at the Llwynypia baths which have now been demolished.

The Workman's Baths, Llwynypia in 1908. The swimming baths were opened by Mr W.W. Hood, immediately after the unveiling of the statue of his father, Archibald Hood, on the Library Green in July 1906. The building of the baths had been a dream of his father who had encouraged its construction by donating the land on which it would be built. The employees of the colliery donated one penny a week from their wages to pay for the building. It was used for the benefit of the local community for many years, until it had to be closed, due to subsidence. The pool was also covered over and used for various social events such as concerts, plays, drama festivals, and when it became a Boys' Club it was used for many sporting activities. Unfortunately, through lack of members it closed and was demolished in the 1980s; a block of flats was later built on the site.

LIBRARY AND MONUMENT. LLWYNYPIA.

The statue of Archibald Hood which was erected in front of the Workman's Institution, Llwynypia, just after the official unveiling by William Abraham (Mabon) MP, in 1906. The cost of the memorial was covered by miners' subscriptions, which gives proof of his popularity, and is a public recognition of his philanthropic interest in the welfare of his workforce.

Glamorgan Colliery, *c.* 1905. Archibald Hood was born in Kilmarnock, Scotland; hence the colliery was familiarly known as the 'Scotch' Colliery. The company sank the Nos 1, 2 and 3 shafts in 1862. One major by-product of the colliery was the production of bricks which amounted to approximately 10,000 a day. They were made by women using hand moulds, with fireclay from the No. 3 pit. The colliery closed in 1945, but certain shafts were left open for many years after, for pumping and ventilation purposes.

Pay Day at the Glamorgan Colliery in 1908. This building was also used as a first aid station and was located on the main Llwynypia to Tonypandy road. This road was usually covered in fine ash from the colliery stacks.

Miners protesting about the use of 'black leg' labour in the power house during the 1910 strike.

The scene after the riot which took place near the power house, in 1910. Note the mounted police and the debris of a wooden fence.

Llwynypia Road in 1908.

Llwynypia railway station, before 'modernization', with the stacks of the 'Scotch' Colliery in the background, *c.* 1895.

114

Llwynypia Road in 1905.

The 'modern' railway station had its own signal box, stationmaster, booking clerks and porters, as well as waiting rooms with coal fires, in 1906.

Stable House, c. 1900. Thomas Collier was born at Penylan, near Cowbridge in 1840. He became the head farrier at the Glamorgan 'Scotch' Colliery, and lived in Stable House. He married Catherine Butler and they had a child which they named Celia. After the death of his first wife, he remarried and his second wife, Charlotte, later gave birth to a girl, Sarah Ann. The photograph shows the family outside the house, from left to right: -?-, Celia Collier, Charlotte Collier, -?-, -?-, Sarah Ann Collier (child), Thomas Collier, -?-.

Glyncornel House in 1904. This was the home of Mr William Walker Hood, general manager of the Glamorgan Coal Company and son of Archibald Hood. It was known locally as 'Old Glycornel' and was the equivalent of the lord of the manor's hall to the residents of Llwynypia. It was replaced by the even more impressive 'New Glyncornel', which was higher up the mountain and was approached by a wide and winding drive through dense woodland. 'New Glyncornel' was built for Mr Leonard W. Llewellyn.

Mr Daniel Thomas Jones was the electrical engineer responsible for the operation of the electrical equipment in the power house during miners' strikes and periods of unemployment. The switchboard had to be manned at all times to ensure that the pumps were working in order to avoid flooding of the colliery workings. He is the father of Owen Vernon Jones who became headmaster of Porth County Grammar School, later the Comprehensive School, and Norman Allen Jones who became the Rhondda's District Education Officer and later headmaster of Tonypandy Comprehensive School.

Sir Leonard Wilkinson Llewellyn KBE was born in Monmouthshire on 11 June 1874. His father was Llewellyn Llewellyn JP, High Sheriff of Monmouthshire. He was educated at Monmouth Grammar School, Cheltenham Private School, and Heidelberg. He became director and general manager of the Cambrian Colliery, as well as being the director of Aberdare Colliery Co. Ltd, Glamorgan Colliery, Fernhill Colliery, Sankey and Sons Ltd, Phoenix Patent Fuel Ltd, Welsh Navigation Colliery Co., Celtic Colliery Ltd, and a number of other large colliery undertakings. He was knighted in 1917, in recognition of his role as controller of non-ferrous metals to the Ministry of Munitions and for his contribution to the war effort. He became High Sheriff of Monmouthshire in 1920, residing at Glen Usk, Caerleon, Monmouthshire. He died on the 13 June 1926 at the age of 52.

Glyncornel Lake, *c*. 1945.

Leonard Llewellyn escorting the Prince of Wales to lunch at Glyncornel Mansion, during his visit in 1919. The new house, built for Sir Leonard, was popularly known as 'The Mansion' to distinguish it from the original agent's residence which became known as 'Lower Glyncornel' or 'Old Glyncornel'.

The Llwynypia Home Guard battalion was based at Bryn Ivor in the 1940s.

St. Cynon's Churchmen's Guild, 1932.

St Cynon's church guild in 1932. The new church was built in 1930 with the original church becoming the church hall. It was demolished in the 1960s, and a block of flats was built on the site.

Sherwood, Llwynypia in 1905. This photograph shows the large Piper and Locke's grocery shop, on the left, which was later known as Piper's. At this time, Sherwood was regarded as being a 'posh' area with its bay windows and forecourts and 'every parlour had a piano'.

Pontrhondda Farm, c. 1906. Around 1907, the roof was blown off the farm which resulted in the farmhouse being demolished. The stables, which were attached to the farmhouse, managed to survive and were used by Mr Oliver Evans, horse trader, and others, until 1955. They were then demolished to make an access road to the newly built Rhondda College of Further Education. The school, to the right of the photograph, was absorbed into the college complex.

The staff at Pontrhondda School in 1931. On the back row, from left to right: Ron Middleton, B. Haddock, ? Davies, George Davies, G. Jones, R. John. On the front row: Blanchard Evans, W.D. Jones, R. Hopkins, I.D. Griffiths, S. Howells, Stan Davies, -?-. The headmaster, Mr Ivor David Griffiths, sat in the middle of the front row, was known locally as 'Ivor Dai'.

Pontrhondda School concert, performing *Hansel and Gretel* in 1951. On the back row, from left to right: Jowie Rhydech, Diane Rocke, Linda Stokes, Pat ?, Wendy Williams, -?-, Pat Davies, Sandra Phelps. On the front row: Michael Glanville, Christine May, Janice Jones, Mike Saunders, Janice Llewellyn.

Members of Pontrhondda School's staff, performing a play in the school in 1940. They were, from left to right: ? Morgans, Harry Nash, Eddie Parry, B.J. Williams, Roger Lewis, Gwyn 'Pancho' Davies, Ieuan Parry, ? Melmeth and 'Tich' Morris.

Pontrhondda Boys' School, Standard 5A, in 1931. The class teacher, centre left, is Mr Reg Hopkins. The young boy standing behind the headmaster, Mr I.D. Griffiths, is Owen Vernon Jones, who became the headmaster of Porth County Grammer School and later Porth County Comprehensive School.

The Homes, Llwynypia in 1923. Built in 1900 by the local Board of Guardians, they were completed in 1904. By 1927, the Homes had been converted into hospital wards and became the first general hospital in the Rhondda.

The Main Square, known as Partridge Square, Llwynypia in 1923.

A view of Llwynypia in 1904. The Glamorgan 'Scotch' Colliery can be seen in the distance. The Pontrhondda School, in the bottom right, became part of the complex of the Rhondda College of Further Education which opened in 1955.

Sports day at Llwynypia and Tonypandy athletic ground in 1884. It has been said that during the winter, Archibald Hood would have the ground flooded and frozen over in order that people could participate in curling matches and ice skating.

Gelligaled Baths, c. 1950. The baths were demolished with the opening of the new sports centre in 1975.

Mr Davies, the shopkeeper of Sherwood, was known locally as Mr Davies Phelps. He opened a Boys' Club in the tin shed attached to the side of his shop in the early 1930s. One of the main events that he organized was a camping trip to Porthcawl which was open to all members of the club. The cost of this trip was 7s a week, which included transport, all food, and of course a tent to sleep in. The photograph shows a group from the club at Newton, Porthcawl, in August 1934. The young boy sitting on the extreme right of the front row is Norman Jones, who in later years became the Director of Education for the Rhondda, and headmaster of Tonypandy Comprehensive School. The boy with arms folded, third from the right, is his brother Vernon, who became headmaster of Porth County School.

Acknowledgements

The author would like to thank the large number of people who helped in the compilation of this book. Without their assistance the book would not have been published. I apologize to anyone whose name has been omitted from the following list: Mr Harry Barnard (Trealaw), Mrs E. Bennett (Pentre), Mr John Charles (Tonypandy), Mrs Coleman and Mrs Williams (Williamstown School), Mrs Davies (Dinas), Mr Terry Davies (Dinas), Mr Gywn Evans (Tonypandy), Mr George Farnham (Trealaw), Miss Kay Warren Morgan and Mrs Stephanie Thomas (Treorchy Library), Mr Glyn Owen (Trealaw), Mr and Mrs Ken Raikes (Trealaw), Mr Keith Ravenhill (Clydach Vale), Mr Bill Richards (Tonypandy), Mr and Mrs Spencer Saint (Penygraig), Mr and Mrs Roy Saunders (Ystrad), Mr Edgar Seale (Trealaw), Mrs Pat Sullivan (Trealaw), Mr Don Taylor (Tonypandy), Mr Gareth Williams (Treorchy). Last, but by no means least, I would like to thank Mr Owen Vernon Jones (Penygraig) for his excellent introduction.